FUNDAMENTAL BOOK
OF SIGIL MAGICK

K.P. Theodore

Erebus Society

First published in Great Britain in 2018
by Erebus Society

First Edition

Copyright of Text © K.P. Theodore 2018
Cover & illustration copyright © Constanin Vaughn 2018

ISBN: 978-1-912461-06-6

www.erebussociety.com

TABLE OF CONTENTS

INTRODUCTION TO SIGILS

Sigils are one of the most efficient practices in Magick. There are different kinds of sigils that are divided by their use in two large groups.

The sigils that are created by a practitioner in order to create mental triggers for certain tasks based on influences or qualities and to aid in magickal workings, are called "Mental Sigils". By the term "Mental Sigils" we refer to all sigils that are used as the visual representation of the practitioner's mindset, will, thoughts, intentions and desired outcome. The term, derives from the Hebrew word הלוגס (segula) which is a word that has the meanings of "property, quality, virtue" and is used to indicate words and/or actions.

The second large group, are the sigils that have a symbolic meaning, not only for the practitioner's (user's) mind, but they also have a meaning and effect in the physical world. These sigils are called "Physical Sigils" and the term derives from the Latin word "sigillum" that has the meanings of "seal, figure, statuette" and is used to indicate the physical representation of an idea. By the term "Physical Sigils" we refer to sigils that are used as the visual and physical representation of ideas, qualities, spirits, and all that is in existence.

These for example are the sigils that have been used in medieval magick grimoires to represent demons, creatures, spells and more.

In detail:

Mental Sigils: are tools that can be used in order to "program" one's brain to function in a certain way. Subconsciously, they stimulate one's desire to achieve a goal and influence their actions so they can act towards it.

To achieve this, one has to register the sigil's meaning in their subconscious mind so they can act and work towards their goal by "instinct" and select the appropriate path and actions that will lead them to the desired outcome.

Examples:

- A practitioner could create a sigil that will influence them to find the will to study every time they see a red ball. Then they can place a red spherical object by their desk, so every time they pass by, subconsciously they get the desire to sit down and study.

- A practitioner might create a sigil that will influence them to become more productive. This can be in general, about their employment or a project etc. So after the sigil has been created and registered, every time they make a thought about the pre-set subject, they are subconsciously influenced to become productive and engaging regarding the subject.

One can meditate on and use a ready made sigil or create their own from scratch if their experience allows it.

Mental sigils have to be registered and activated through specific techniques in order to function properly.

Physical Sigils: also called "Seals of Power", are symbols that are created and used to carry a property/influence within them so they can be used in the physical world and/or create changes in it.

These symbols gain their power from the collective consciousness of their user's, as they are catholic symbols, used widely among occultists and occult practices. Examples of these type of symbols are the cross, the pentacle, the ouroboros etc.

Physical sigils have also been designed in such a way that their "physique" (shape and form) resembles their physical properties. For further details on the physiology of sigils, you can research how certain shapes are connected with certain emotions, research the psychological meanings of everyday shapes and forms and their resemblance to ideas, and also observe the shapes or symbols that are used to represent ideas in traditions around the world.

On the contrary to mental sigils, physical sigils have to be placed physically on the target.

Examples:

- A practitioner could carve a sigil of power on a tool that is used for magickal workings to imbue it with certain properties and/or amplify its potency.

- They could paint a warding sigil on the back side of a door or window to avert unwanted energies, beings etc.

- One could wear a clarity sigil as a talisman in the form of a necklace during meditation or other workings for a clearer focus and thinking.

Physical sigils don't have to be registered through a technique as mental sigils do. The use of these sigils alone is enough to register them in the subconscious mind and link them to the grid of collective consciousness. Although one is free to meditate on them, use them as mental sigils and experiment further.

For a better understanding, think of the previous examples of the cross and the pentacle. When someone uses the cross as a protective talisman, they do not need to meditate on it and register its use through a technique. The belief on the cross is what makes it function. In the same way, when a practitioner uses a pentacle to enforce their magickal workings, knowing that the pentacle is used for certain purposes and that it has certain qualities is enough for it to work as expected.

The catholic belief or knowledge about a certain thing or idea is what gives them their properties, their meaning and their power. If we accept as true that "consciousness creates reality", then it is simple to understand that magick itself is a way of manipulating and altering reality through the power of will. This in its turn makes it easy to understand the ways in which magickal techniques can create changes in the physical world and finally comprehend how catholic/widespread symbols and collective consciousness work.

Activating or "registering" a mental sigil is simply a way of implanting an idea in the subconscious mind, in order to be connected with the collective consciousness and gain a true value, exist, and in its turn work in one's mind and give results in the physical world. The seals of power or physical sigils, their properties and what they represent, have already been accepted in the same way that a group of people accepts factual knowledge, thus they already exist in the grid of collective consciousness.

CREATING THE SIGILS

There are many different reasons why someone might want to use sigils and unfortunately not all of them can be covered in a single book. Personality, circumstances and other parameters might make it impractical to use a generic sigil.

For that reason, practitioners can create and use their own custom sigils that are tailored to meet their exact needs. It takes knowledge, effort and determination to create the perfect sigil but practice makes perfect.

There are many different kinds of sigils and a lot of different methods that can be used to create each type, but the two most common types/methods of sigils are the "Letter" and the "Pictorial" sigils or methods.

Both are as effective as the other as long as the intent is clear and the activation techniques are followed properly.

THE WORD METHOD

Letter sigils are based on words. To create a sigil, one must clearly express their true intent in the form of a sentence. It is also important to express the intent not as a wish for the future, but as if it is something that has been already achieved.

For example, if one wants to be more courageous, they should not express is at "I wish I have more courage" but instead, it should be expressed as "I have the courage I need".

Once the intent has been expressed accordingly and has been made into a sentence, all duplicate letters must be removed. The easiest way of doing so is by reading each word letter by letter and every time a letter appears more than one time, simply cross it out.

For example:

I HAVE THE COURAGE
I NEED

By doing so, only unique letters are left, which means that only unique shapes and sounds can be produced. This is important for two reasons.

First if all, when creating a letter sigil, it gives a sense of uniqueness in each shape, this is because each letter of the alphabet is quite different to the others. In its turn, this means that when creating the visual sigil, one pays more attention on how to place each letter and put a bit more effort while doing so.

It is also best to do so for phonetic sigils as it is much easier to use non-repetitive sounds when it comes to programming the brain. Even though we use mantras in activation techniques such as the "Mantrical Activation" it is always best that the mantras are build on words and sentences that are made of unique letters.

After deleting the duplicate letters from the sentence, what is left are the unique letters in their original order.

I HAVETCOURGND

Sigils though work by being "absorbed" in the depths of our subconscious mind, and to do so, they should be easy to forget. Having the letters in their original order is a good reminder of what the original sentence used to be which is not helpful to achieve the desired effect.

To eliminate this obstacle, the letters have to be rearranged. This can be either at a completely random order or one might choose to create new words out of these letters, words that sound appealing to the practitioner.

For example:

GIDU CHORVENTA

In that way, the original sentence of intent "I have the courage I need" has been transformed to " Gidu Chorventa". It is best if the newly formed words don't resemble any other known words or sigils to the practitioner, as it would be much easier to avoid random connections and to make it sink in the subconscious mind.

Once this has been achieved, the visual sigil's making process can begin. To do so, simply take the letters, one at a time, and place them together so they can form a new image, one that does not resemble letters or the original intention. The letters can be placed next to each other or on top of each other etc. Additional adornments such as dots, crosses, tails, stars etc. can be used once the letters have been placed, for a more aesthetically pleasing outcome.

Feel free to play around and experiment with various different forms of the same sigil before you settle to the one that works best.

The "Courage" sigil, Gidu Chorventa.

For a better understanding on how these letters formed the sigil, here follows a step by step representation of the process. The thin lines are the complete sigil and the bold lines are the shapes that represent each letter.

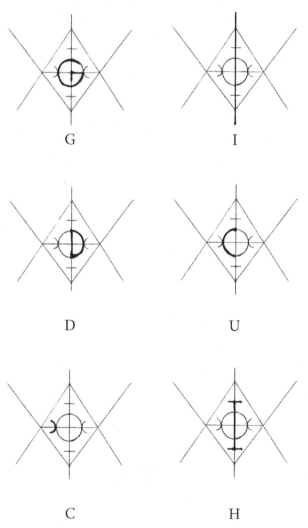

G

I

D

U

C

H

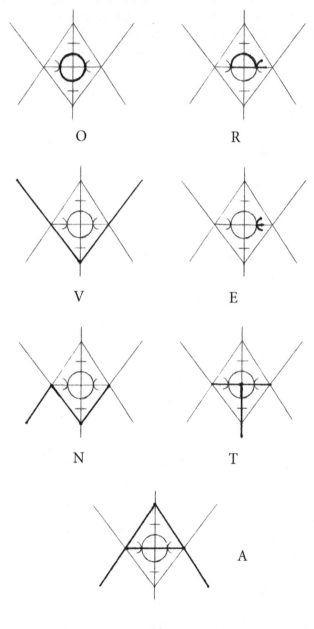

O

R

V

E

N

T

A

At this point it is quite apparent that letters can be rotated, turned upside down, flip horizontally and manipulated in any way.

This gives a lot of creative freedom and also makes the sigil more effective as the lines are easier to be forgotten and thus sink in the subconscious mind during the activation process.

THE PICTORIAL METHOD

In the pictorial method, one creates a visual representation of their true intention to begin with. Using the same example of the "Courage" sigil, the basic form of the sentence "I have the courage I need" in the pictorial method should be an image, which for the practitioner, represents courage.

Most people associate courage with a warrior, so for this example, the basic form of the pictorial sigil could be this:

A brave warrior whose core is their heart, and they are equipped with a mighty sword to represent the "bravery" in taking action and a shield to represent the "courage" in being resilient and not giving up.

The next step in forming the sigil is to simplify the original drawing into a more plain version, one that can be expressed with simple lines and shapes. Taking away any "volume" and simply depicting the form's structure that lies underneath.

For example:

Now that the visual representation has been stripped down to its basic core, it is time to start altering the form. To do so, start by shifting any loose ends towards the centre of the image in order to make it look a bit more solid.

For example:

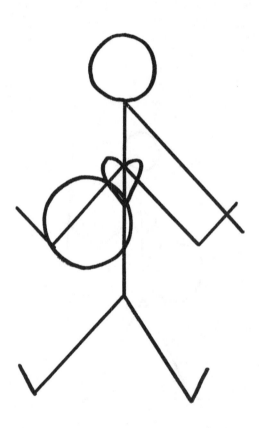

The next step of the process is to distort the form completely based on the existing elements, so it does no longer resemble the original image which in this case is a humanoid figure with a sword, a shield and a visible heart.

To do so, the easiest and most efficient way is to shift the existing shapes, move them around, rotate, overlap them and change their size. For example:

The final step of the process, is to refine the current outcome into the final form of the sigil. This is done by repeating the previous step again but this time, lines and shapes can be removed and decorations can be added.

For example, the shape that used to be the head has been enlarged and merged with what used to be the shield. What used to be the limbs have been joined to form a more prominent and geometric structure and so on.

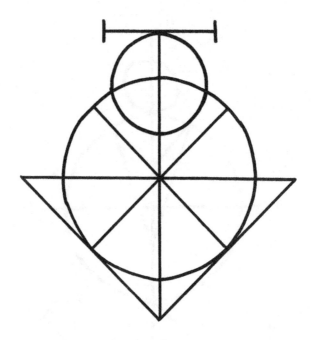

And this is what the finished sigil of the pictorial method looks like. A form that does not resemble the original drawing but still inspires a sense of boldness and confidence.

ACTIVATING A SIGIL

There are various ways in which one can register and activate a mental sigil. From physical pain and exhaustion to orgasm an ecstasy, the range of techniques is vast as people experiment and in the end, practitioners tend to develop their own personal technique.

A basic way to start the journey of sigil magick, although not the easiest one, is to learn how to register and activate sigils through a series of techniques based on meditation and banishing.

The Procedure:

Phase 1 – The Preparation:

Before you start make sure that you have everything you need in order to complete the process without any interruptions. This means the location that the practice will take place, any clothing, tools such as candles and incense that you might want to use in order to achieve a certain mental state (or simply because you like to work this way), the sigil etc. This also includes any non magickal chores that you need to do before starting to make sure that none will interrupt you or contact you, no animals or pets will bother you and that nothing will go off (such as an alarm, reminder etc.) during the process.

Find a space suitable for meditation and once you are fully prepared proceed to the next phase.

Phase 2 – Targeted Meditation:

Find a very comfortable position, either sitting or standing, place the sigil in front of you, close your eyes and start emptying your mind. To do so, you need to "meditate-not", "think nothing" and let all of your thoughts flow away and disappear from your mind. Do not think of the next phase, what you are doing at the moment or why you are doing it. Just relax, let go and feel the light sensation and peaceful feeling of emptiness.

Once you achieve this, open your eyes and fixate your attention on the sigil (it helps to place the sigil on a plank of wood or other similar object and have it level with the hight of your face). Think of the reason you created it, think of its meaning, its qualities, properties and purpose.

Now start meditating on the goal of the process and the reason you have this specific sigil in front of you. It is important not to do the meditation as a wish. Do not wish for the result you want, instead, feel it as if you have already achieved it. If your goal is for example to become more productive, do not wish for more productivity. See yourself being productive as if you already are. Meditate and envision that you have achieved your goal.

Phase 3 – Suppressive Meditation:

Close your eyes and empty your mind completely again in the same way that has been mentioned in the previous phase.

Once you feel that your mind is completely empty of thoughts again, open your eyes and concentrate on the sigil's shape and lines, this time, without thinking of its meaning at all. See its physical-visual form as if it is something meaningless to you.

At this point you can use the mantra of the sigil (if it has one) as an aid. Mantras help silence the mind as the repetition of the same word or words in a quiet and monotonous fashion, tranquilises the brain and dumbs the mind's systems that are responsible for creative thinking, which makes us think of the past, the future and the endless possibilities and scenarios that are the cause of stress and anxiety. Thus, mantras can help to deal with abstract thoughts and bring the mind a step closer to a timeless present, free from thoughts, wishes, expectations and burden.

<u>Phase 4 – Absorbing the Sigil:</u>

Keep facing the sigil, close your eyes and hold your breath for as long as possible. Hold the air in, till you can't physically bare it any longer. The moment you feel that holding your breath has become agonising, exhale. As you inhale, open your eyes and look at the sigil. When you have enough air in your lungs again, close your eyes and repeat the process.

Repeat this again and again to the point of near exhaustion, every time have your eyes closed during air deprivation and only open them to look at the sigil as you inhale and take another breath to keep you conscious.

During this phase, you can add an additional anguish factor and level of difficulty, by standing in a very uncomfortable and strenuous pose as you do the breathing process. Physical exertion has been used since the dawn of time when people wanted to achieve certain mental states, experience ecstasy, find nirvana etc.

19

Examples of poses are:

- Standing on the tips of your toes throughout the whole process.

- Laying on the ground and maintaining the V position. Only the gluteal region (posterior) should touch the ground, as the torso, arms and legs are extended upwards so the full body can create a V shape formation.

You can also explore yoga for more inspiration regarding poses such as :

- Ardha Navasana – half boat pose.

- Malasana – garland pose.

- Tittibhasana – firefly pose.

Avoid poses that are upside down (feet up, head down) such as:

- Adho Mukha Vrksasana – handstand pose.

- Pincha Mayurasana – feathered peacock pose.

- Salamba Sarvangasana – shoulderstand pose.

As these will increase blood pressure on the head and combined with the oxygen deprivation it is very likely that will make you faint.

Phase 5 – Banishing the Sigil:

The final step of this procedure is the banishing. This, will push the sigil in your subconscious mind and lock it there so it can start working.

To do so, first burn or destroy the sigil in any other way. Then the most simple way in which you can "break" the connection between your conscious mind and the sigil is to laugh. Abrupt laughter is considered to be one of the most easy and effective ways to banish a sigil.

Just laugh, loudly and for no other reason. As you laugh think of something else, anything that is not related with your goal, sigils, magick etc. It can be a moment of the past, an imaginary situation, even an object.

As soon as you finish laughing, get up (if you were on the ground), move away from the place you were practicing immediately, and start doing something else, something completely different. For example, if you were activating the sigil in the living room, leave the room and go to the kitchen to eat or organise the pantry etc.

After you have activated a sigil it is better not to return to any magickal related workings for the rest of the day, until you go to sleep and wake up the next day. Distract yourself with mundane chores or socialise with people. The more you forget about the sigil (visual appearance and purpose) the more it will sink in your subconscious mind and the better it will work to bring the desired results.

Mantrical Sigil Activation:

The Mantrical Sigils (or Phonetic Sigils) can be activated through a very simple, single step technique. To do so, repeat the mantra in a monotonous fashion over and over again for as long as possible, from many minutes to a few hours. The longer the repetition period takes, the better.

The purpose of this, is to use the monotonous sounds to make the conscious mind focus on the acoustic part of the sigil, so its actual meaning can be internalised subconsciously and bypass both conscious and subconscious minds in order for the idea/porpose to be seeded in the unconscious mind.

In both, Visual (word/pictorial method) and Mantrical activation techniques, the procedure aims to implant the sigil's meaning in the unconscious mind, like a seed, so it can "bloom" in it, and grow and flourish in the subconscious mind. The subconscious mind in its turn can use this as a form of motivation and suggestion in order to influence the conscious mind, which in its turn will put all this into actions towards achieving the end goal.

Note: Physical exertion can be incorporated in this technique as well. To do so, repeat the mantrical method while staying in one of the poses mentioned in the previous technique (Visual Sigils).

PRONUNCIATION GUIDE

The correct pronunciation and accent used in a mantra are very important, as they affect the final sound that is repeated over and over, thus, they affect the final frequency. Different frequencies affect the brain in different ways.

The following is a brief guide to the correct pronunciation by the use of a standard pronunciation key, in order to approach the desired sound outcome as much as possible.

VOWELS:

Respelling Symbols	Examples	IPA Symbols
a	gap	/æ/
aw	bought	/ɔː/
e	dress	/ɛ/
i	mirror	/Ir/
o	plot	/ɒ/
ow	shouth	/aʊ/
u	boot	/ʊ/
y	*same as* **i**	

CONSONANTS:

Respelling Symbols	Examples	IPA Symbols
b	**b**at	/b/
c	**c**ar	/k/
d	**d**o	/d/
f	**f**ire	/f/
g	**g**et	/g/
h	**h**ero	/h/
j	**g**in, **j**am	/dʒ/
k	kno**ck**	/k/
l	**l**and	/l/
m	**m**ountain	/m/
n	**n**ear	/n/
ng	ma**ng**le, ri**ng**	/ŋ/
p	**p**in	/p/
r	**r**eal	/r/
s	**s**eeker	/s/
t	**t**owel	/t/
v	**v**iper	/v/
w	**w**e, q**u**ick	/w/
z	**z**ip	/z/

For the correct pronunciation of the mantras, one should avoid using their native (especially native English) accent.

Mantras have to be pronounced in a very plain, almost hard accent. One can use as an example the way the consonants are pronounced in Russian. For example R is always very hard and sharp, same goes for T and B etc. For the vowels , one can think of the way vowels are pronounced in Italian. Always very clear and sharp without any of the fading sounds that other languages such as English have at the end of a vowel.

Note: It is advised to listen to recordings in Latin or Ancient Greek in order to fully comprehend the accents given.

Physical Sigil Activation

For the Physical Sigils, the best activation technique is to "take care" of their meaning while using them. To do so, you need to concentrate on their qualities and purpose as you are placing them on the materials/objects of your choice.

For the Physical Sigils there is no need to meditate on them, register and banish them as in other activation techniques, although some practitioners choose to. This is subject on personal preference.

Examples for materials that sigils can be placed upon are: paper, cloth, clay, stone, wood, metal, skin etc.

Examples for objects that sigils can be placed upon are: daggers, wands, clothes, doors, floor, jewellery etc.

Note: Physical Sigils can also be used in the form of tattoos, especially for placing qualities and enchantments in one's self. If you choose to do so, make sure that you have a really good reason, select the most appropriate sigil and use non synthetic pigments.

MENTAL SIGILS

The Mental Sigils in this book, are a selection of basic sigils that are useful to most beginners (and not only) in sigil magick.

On each page, you will find the Sigil in its visual form, the name of the sigil, its properties, its mantrical form and in some sigils, notes and suggestions. Underneath the text there is space to take your own notes, describe thoughts or record the results you achieved with each sigil.

Sigils for the Mind

TO AID FOCUSING

This sigil can be used when you need to focus on a specific subject, goal, task etc. It can be used in a combination of sigils or in its own.

Mantra: GAWN SCODI FTUH

Notes:

FOR CONCENTRATION

This sigil is to be used when you need to improve your concentration in general. It is better not to use it for a specific target or task as it might limit your general concentration and make it feel "narrow".

Mantra: OMPRI VENTAC

Notes:

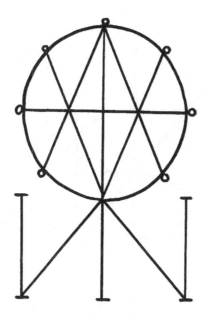

FOR MEDITATION

Use this sigil for when you want to meditate. Use is just before meditation to to make the following meditation session more efficient or use it at any other time to help improve your meditation technique and state of mind in general.

Mantra: VERPIM TANDO

Notes:

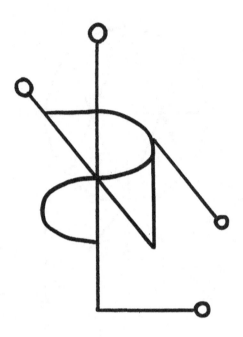

FOR RELAXATION

This sigil can be used in order to help you relax in a certain moment, or as a general practice of relaxation . To get the better results, meditate on this sigil and use it frequently to improve your general state of tension and become more relaxed overall.

Once you use it for general improvement, you can then use it for more specific and targeted occasions. To do so, bring the sigil's effect in mind (without thinking of its visual form) and meditate momentarily in the desired outcome which is to feel the lightness of being relaxed.

Mantra: DIX ARMEL

Notes:

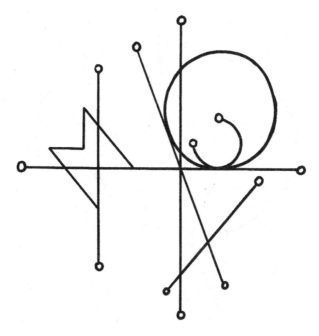

FOR CLEAR THOUGHTS

Use this sigil in order to make things easier to "see". This sigil is to be used for the general improvement of the thinking process in all matters and subjects. It helps define, categorise and brighten the thoughts so the frustration during thinking and contemplating can be eliminated.

Mantra: PYCT FOWHI NARGLEM

Notes:

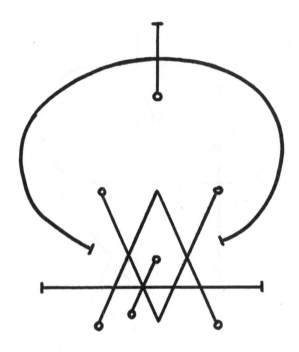

FOR CLARITY

This is a sigil that aids to improve general clarity in one's mind and thoughts. From observing, to thinking and ana-lysing , to making a decision, it can help make each process separately and all together, easier and more efficient.

Mantra: THEVA CIRLY

Notes:

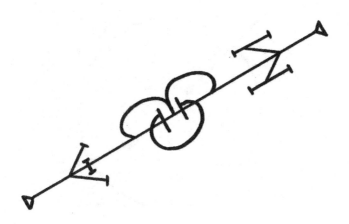

MENTAL BANISHING

Banishing is one of the most common practices in ritual magick. This sigils helps to make banishing ritual more efficient and to maintain a healthy mentality during rituals.

Mantra: GINTA BELMSH

Notes:

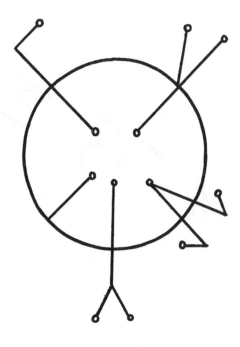

MEMORY

This is a sigil to aid in memory work. It can be used in general for meditations and techniques that aim to affect memory. Because each sigil can carry a single message in the subconscious, use it only for one goal. This means that you can use it for either improving your memory, worsen your memory, to remember or forget something, or to affect your memory in any other way, but choose only one of the above.

Using the same sigil for multiple goals, will make it in-effective and might cause a confusion in the activation process.

Mantra: OM ERY GNAL

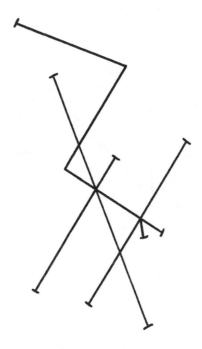

RITUAL MINDSET

Use this sigil to make it easier to achieve the ritual mindset. Activate the sigil once, and if successful, this will aid you in finding the proper ritual mindset in an easier way, with less preparation and better efficiency before you take part in a ritual.

Mantra: MEDTAR LINUS

Notes:

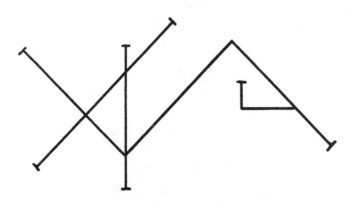

SPELL MINDSET

Use this sigil to make it easier to achieve the magickal mindset you need during a spell. As with the "Ritual Mindset" sigil, activate this sigil once and if successful, this will aid you in finding the proper magickal-spell mindset in an easier way, with less preparation and better efficiency before you work on or cast a spell.

Mantra: CANDTIP SGELM

Notes:

Sigils for one's Self

FOR MOTIVATION

This sigil is to be used in order to find a goal driven attitude and become more motivated. It can be used either on its own, to promote motivation in general or in a combination with another sigil and/or technique in order to focus and direct the motivation towards a specific goal.

Mantra: MORBING TVAO

Notes:

TO FIND PRODUCTIVITY

Use this sigil in order to become a more productive person. As you activate it, it is helpful to think of the reasons that you want to be productive for.

Do not aim this sigil towards a specific target/goal, instead use it to find productivity in general, and then use your productivity in the work you wish.

Mantra: BERCOMP DVUTI

Notes:

TO INCREASE PRODUCTIVITY

If you are a productive person or if you have already activated the "Productivity Sigil" and you need to become even more productive, then use this sigil.

This will work in ways to enhance the existing "productivity" mindset, therefore, do not use it if you are not productive to begin with.

If you are not sure about the level of productivity you want to achieve, then you can try another sigil to help you follow your current task.

Mantra: ESPOR NICA DYVTU

Notes:

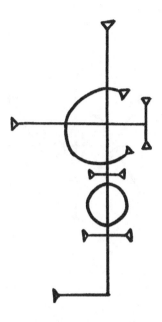

TO SET A GOAL

Use this sigil if you have trouble making a start and/or focusing on a specific target.

While you activate this sigil, have the goal you want to set in mind and think of the reasons you want to set this specific goal.

Alternatively, you can activate it as you meditate on your ability to set goals and/or focusing on targets, in order to influence your decision-making process and your attention span , so you can achieve this in general and not only for a specific goal.

Mantra: PEL GHASTO

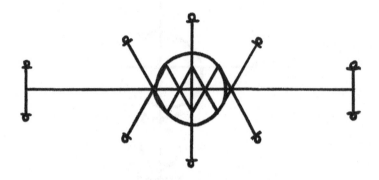

TO FOLLOW A GOAL

If you have set a goal or if you already have activated the "Set a Goal" sigil, you can use this sigil to help you follow your goal and to avoid any deviations.

This sigil can be used in a combination with the "Motivation" and "Productivity" sigils as an overal aid that is ideal for students, researchers and people who have multiple projects and obligations.

Mantra: LAWNT HEI GOF

Notes:

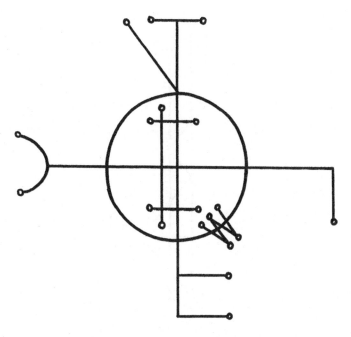

TO FOLLOW A ROUTINE

This sigil is to aid with following daily and repetitive tasks, such as waking up at a certain time, remembering a small errand, and following a daily schedule.

Before you activate the sigil, gather all the information you want to add to your schedule. During the activation, meditate in the tasks, their order, the timetables and visualise yourself already living Successfully in this schedule.

Mantra: LWITH NUG FERO

Notes:

47

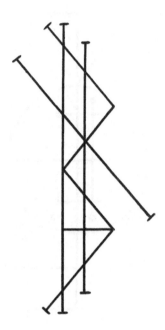

TO WORK HARDER

Use this sigil if you already have the motivation to work on a certain task, but you lack the mental endurance.

Lack of mental endurance means that you lack the ability to be determined in your goal when things get more difficult, that you give up if the first try is not successful or that you avoid pushing yourself going a step further, which has a result that you never achieve your true potential.

Activate this sigil after you have set goals, as this sigil works in general, in your attitude and mentality, rather than on specific targets and in order for it to function properly you need to have a set desire, targets and goals you need to work on.

Mantra: DHAWR KEMO

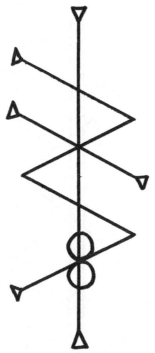

TO LEARN A NEW SKILL

If you have already made the choice to learn a new skill, this sigil can aid with influencing your mind to absorb practical knowledge in a faster pace and in a more efficient manner.

This sigil works by altering the way your adult mind registers new facts and details, and make it simulate a more child like learning process in which your brain will "absorb" newly introduced information "like a sponge".

Mantra: NAWRGIS KEL

Notes:

49

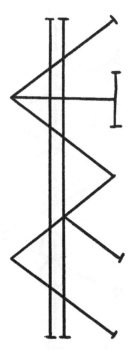

TO STUDY HARDER

In a similar fashion to the "Work Harder" sigil, this one works as an aid in order to direct the existing motivation in an existing goal and maintain the mental durability to the task.

This sigil helps to focus your mind during the studying process and to eliminate any distractions that could cause you to stop while studying.

Because this sigil works on the existing mindset of studying and enhances to focus and determination, activate it after you have started studying a subject.

Mantra: KESTHUR MADY

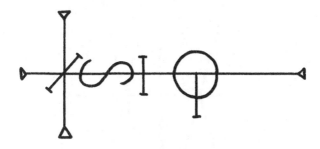

ENGAGEMENT TO TASKS

Use this sigil in order to become more determined when it comes to tasks and chores and to awaken a more engaging nature.

This sigil should not be aimed at specific tasks, routines, and chores or in certain types of tasks, such as workings, learning, creating etc. In the contrary, only use this sigil to empower your engagement in general.

As you activate this sigil, do not thing of any specific goals that you might have, instead focus in your ability to engage with anything, your will to pursue your goals and a broad sense of persistence.

Mantra: NEH GAITOSK

51

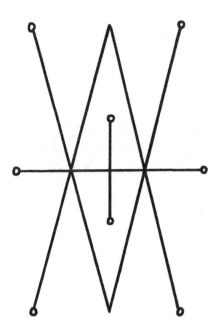

TO BE MORE ACTIVE

Use this sigil in order to "program" your mind to function properly for an active lifestyle. This could be for any reason and any kind of lifestyle that one wants to promote activity in it. This sigil works by creating a dynamic agility in one's mind, thus turning one more active overall, bringing some sense of euphoria and the feeling that there is much energy to be spent on tasks.

To target the effects of this sigil on a specific task or working, you can combine it with the sigil that is made to increase productivity, while working on the subject.

Mantra: VECTIBA

Notes:

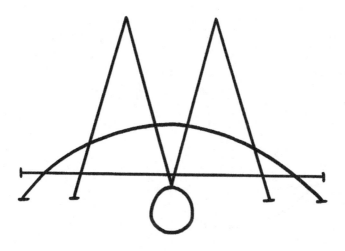

TO BE MORE DARING

The use of this sigil helps the practitioner to become more daring and taking some risks that they normally wouldn't proceed with. This helps to ease the "voices" of doubt and uncertainty that lie in everyone's mind, and in this was it makes it easie to make a choice and step forward in a risky situation.

It is not advised to use this sigil in combination with other sigils that promote courage, strength etc. as this can make one overestimate their own strength and take risks that they can't deal with.

Mantra: DRACOM NIGBE

Notes:

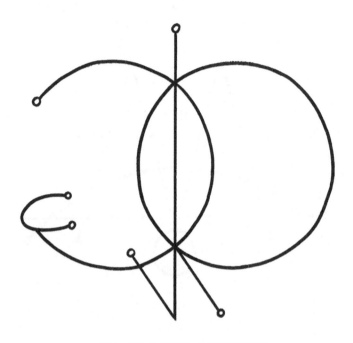

TO BE MORE GENEROUS

Use this sigil when you have the need to be more giving. This could apply to many situations. For example, when moving houses one might need to give away some of their belongings that they feel too attached with. In another situation one might need to be freed from the materialistic needs and offer what they have but not really need to others who are in real need.

This also applies in non-materialistic situations. For example during a friendship or a romantic relationship, one might be too "inaccessible" and distant and have the need to offer more to their friend or partner in a mental and emotional way.

Mantra: GARNEO UMIS

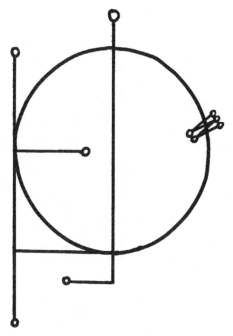

TO BE MORE PEACEFUL

Use this sigil in order to promote tranquility and calmness in one's inner self.

This is a quiet versatile sigil, as it can be used in a variety of different situations. It can be used for long-term purposes when one is already calm to promote an ever more calm and peaceful state of mind, free from distractions and influences of aggravation and annoyance. It can be used as a temporary solution when one is upset, in order to calm down and release any tension. It can be used as a "treatment" when one has the need to change their stress levels and lead a more calm and grounded lifestyle, and so on.

Mantra: FELAC PUMI

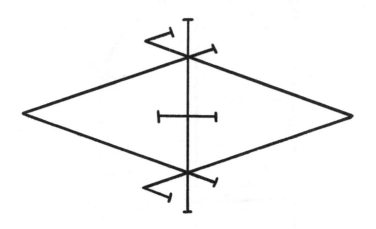

TO BE MORE SENSITIVE

This is a sigil for when one wants to promote the increase of personal sensitivity.

Do not confuse this sigil with other sigils that aim to increase a "senses" based sensitivity. This one is solely for the purpose of emotional based sensitivity. In other words, it does not work in a way to amplify one's physical and psychic senses, but it works by aiding one's emotional intelligence to improve and become more sensitive in "feeling" their or others' emotional state.

Mantra: VENTA MIS

Notes:

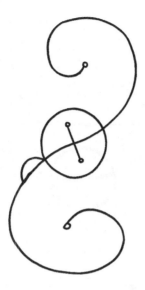

TO BE MORE STABLE

This is another versatile sigil, that can be used to promote one's stability. It can be used for both mental and emotional stability in different ways.

For example, when it comes to mental stability, one can use this sigil to promote stability for a more efficient decision making process or to stabilise their mind once they have made a decision or have expressed an opinion on a subject.

On an emotional level, one can use this sigil to stabilise their current emotional state. For example, after using a technique, sigil or in any means has managed to achieve a desirable emotional state, the sigil can be used as a "fixative" to prolong or maintain the current state.

Mantra: IB CELMO SAT

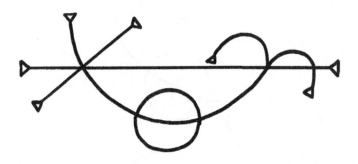

TO BE MORE SYSTEMATIC

This sigil is to be used as an aid to one's practice to become more organised and methodical.

The difference of this sigil in comparison to others, is that it can (or is better) to be registered multiple times during the course of the practice/process. For example, one can create a ten day schedule and repeat the sigil learning process once a day for ten days etc.

The process makes the sigil learning technique a bit different as it can only be banished properly once, on the last time that it is used, but think of it as a simple extension of the learning process over a prolonged period of time.

Mantra: CRAST OMY EI

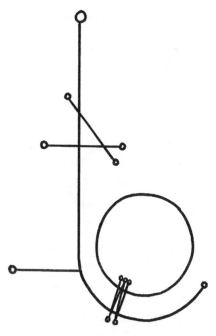

TO BE MORE JOYFUL

Use this sigil when in need to improve the current emotional state.

The use of the sigil does not promote the feeling of joy automatically, instead, it enables the ability for one to become more aware of the positive side of the current situation(s) and influences the thinking process in a healthy way in order to promote favourable scenarios.

Positive thinking, along with recognition and appreciation of the current beneficial elements in combination with an optimistic mentality for the future, is what can make an individual to feel happy.

Manta: YJAMO ULIF

TO OBTAIN BETTER EATING HABITS

This sigil can amplify one's effort towards better eating habits by helping them accept a new diet in a more easy way, and sticking to the new dietary plan.

As with every sigil is important to remember that if one wants to successfully "program" their subconscious mind, they should visualise the desirable outcome as if it is already achieved. Therefore, during tha activation process of the sigil, do not think of the struggles and of the change that has to be achieved, think that every obstacle has been dealt with and that the final change has already been achieved.

Mantra: MAKHET SGOR BINC

Notes:

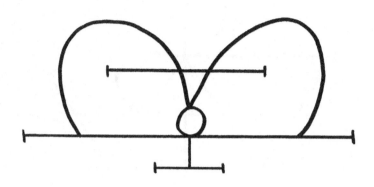

TO BE HEALTHIER

This sigil is to be used in order to obtain healthier habits and adapt to an overall healthy lifestyle.

It works by helping one to overcome the struggles of change and to be more accepting on new personal choices and routines.

As an addition to this sigil, one can also use the sigil that deals with better eating habits, as diet I an essential part of a healthy day to day life.

Mantra: COMBE HALTIR

Notes:

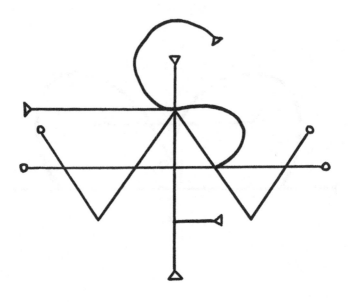

TO SLEEP MORE EASILY

Use this sigil if you goint to sleep at night is more trouble than pleasure.

The most common reason that one might face a difficulty while goint to sleep, is over-thinking. Over-thinking problems, acts of the past, options of the future ad more.

This sigil helps to reduce the amount of night-thoughts and increase the comfort levels in order to relax and fall asleep easier than usual.

It can be used for a few nights in a row before the final banishing is performed, as its physical shape is an aid that helps one to tamper with the brain centers that manage stress, hyperactivity and problem-solving.

Mantra: LHEMP FASIR

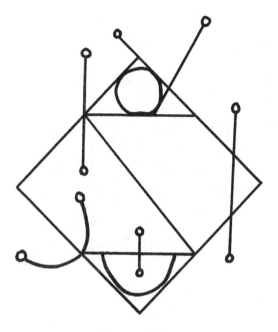

TO ACKNOWLEDGE ONE'S TRUE SELF

This sigile helps one to reach deep within their mind, discover their inner self and acknowledge their true nature. It is a very important technique because finding one's true self means that they find their true purpose, their true will. As they say in the thelemic (and not only) orders "Do what thou wilt shall be the whole of the law". Which briefly translates to "Act based on your true will (one's true nature) and this is what determines what is the law for oneself". It does not matter if one is "good" or "bad" according to others, the only thing that matters is for one to be true to themselves.

For the proper use of this sigil, use it daily for a few days as you meditate and once you have achieved a satisfying degree of self-exploration, perform the banishing.

Mantra: KLEM DOGRAW TUSYF

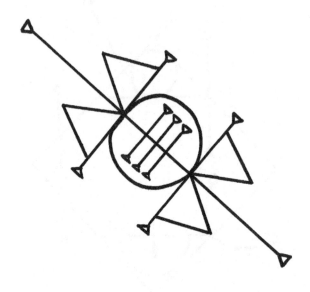

TO ACKNOWLEDGE ONE'S BAD HABITS

This sigil is a very important aid to one's journey of finding their true self. The first step to self-development and to move towards a better future, is to know what lies deep in oneself. The biggest drawback in one's personality is their bad habits. By identifying them and acknowledging the issues, one can move horward and find ways to deal with and manage what is the true obstacle.

Use this sigil while in a very deep meditative state, preferable after the sigil to "acknowledge one's true self" has been used, and use it only once. The repeated use if this sigil is discouraged, as facing the habits again and again might result to compromisation.

Mantra: GOLM HAKT DWEB YSI

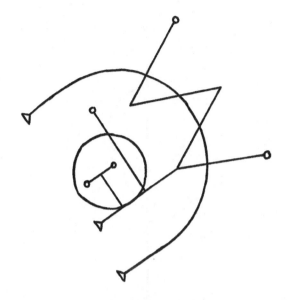

TO MANAGE ONE'S BAD HABITS

Once the sigil to identify and acknowledge the bad habits, one can proceed with the sigil of management.

During the meditation, discover what is the real cause of the bad habits and search for new ways to manage them efficiently, overcome, and if possible, eradicate them.

This sigil can be used in a combination of sigils. Suggested order of use is (a sigil per day for the total of eight days):

To Acknowledge one's True Self
To Acknowledge one's True Self
To Acknowledge one's Bad Habits
To Acknowledge one's True Self
To Acknowledge one's True Self
To Manage one's Bad Habits
To Acknowledge one's True Self
To Acknowledge one's True Self

Mantra: SHAMBYC GENTID

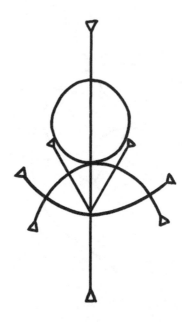

TO BECOME MORE CONSCIOUS

This sigil is to be used in order to increase one's attention and become more conscious.

The level of consciousness on this level, is the consciousness regarding the surrounding environment. The purpose is to become aware of one's "space", see, hear, feel and identify the nature of things, acknowledge the different situations and get an overall better understanding in both physical and mental means.

Mantra: CORM BE NISU

Notes:

FOR EMOTIONAL RELIEF

Use this sigil when there is an emotional Burden. It could be sorrow, grief, worry or even the general unhappiness that comes with the over-thinking process.

It can also be used for emotional relief when the subject is emotions caused by positivity, such as joy and excitement.

Mantra: NEID VOM LYRAT

Notes:

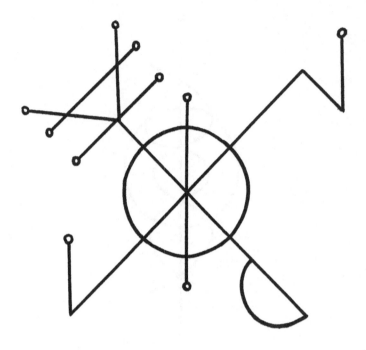

FOR EMOTIONAL INDEPENDENCE

This sigil can be used to alleviate the sense of "dependence". It can be the feeling of depending in a situation, an object, a person, a place etc.

It is a great addition to spells and rituals that deal with freedom, empowerment and severing cords.

Mantra: TANEI MOLDYP

Notes:

68

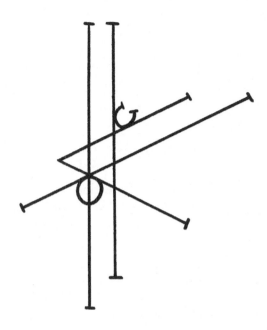

TO AID ONE'S PERCEPTION

When the understanding of situations seems to be dull, or when one needs to get a better understanding of important matters, use this sigil to improve perception in general.

Mantra: VAHTIP BERCON

Notes:

Sigils for Protection

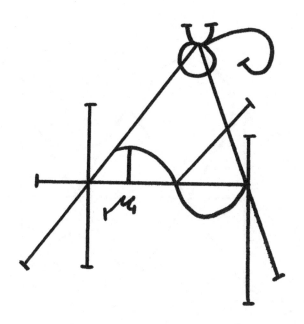

FOR GENERAL PROTECTION

This sigil is a great addition to spells and rituals that deal with protective enchantments. It provides the mind with an additional focus in the "protective mindset" and makes such techniques more effective.

It can also work on its own as a standalone technique.

Mantra: DRAMLOC PITHEG

Notes:

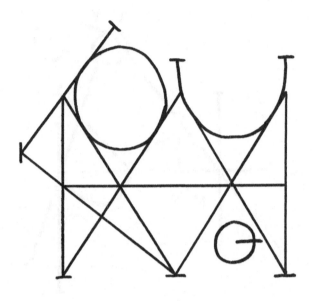

PROTECTION FROM NIGHTMARES

Use this sigil when suffering from night terrors, bad sleep, or the issues that cause sleep paralysis.

While registering this sigil, think of your ideal sleep state and the peaceful feeling that comes with it.

Mantra: GHRASFEM PICTO

Notes:

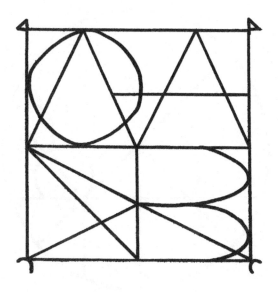

PROTECTION FROM EVENTS OF BAD LUCK

This sigil can be used to prevent unlucky events. It can work in two ways. Either prevent the used from making a bad decision thus preventing the negative event, or help the user "foresee" such event in order to avoid it in the future.

Mantra: FEMBAN DRIKT PULCO

Notes:

PROTECTION FROM BAD DECISIONS

When prone to making bad decisions, use this sigil to help avoid such situations. This sigil works by causing the user to "over-think" certain situations that might cause a future disaster.

Mantra: CROMPTIS FDEBAN

Notes:

Sigils for Power

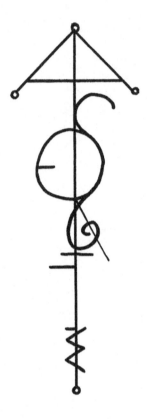

TO RAISE POWER

Use this sigil to raise power in a more efficient way for magickal workings or other techniques.

Overuse of this sigil can cause mental and physical exertion and create a form of addiction to the user.

Mantra: FERTIS POGNAW

Notes:

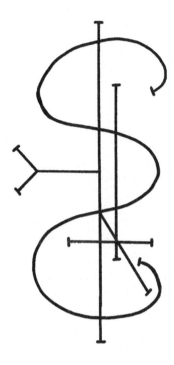

TO ENHANCE ONE'S ABILITIES

This sigil can be used to amplify or make one's natural abilities more efficient. It works especially well with mental abilities that have to do with energy work or the powers of the mind.

Mantra: STRENYM BLICHAD

Notes:

Sigils for Divination

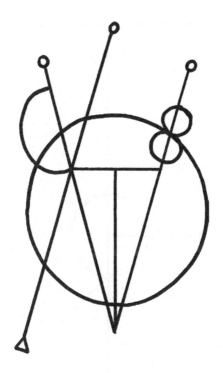

AID FOR DIVINATION IN GENERAL

This sigil is a great way to prepare before an important divination work. It helps clear the mind and provide more accurate visions and interpretations.

Mantra: VANDOT BIS

Notes:

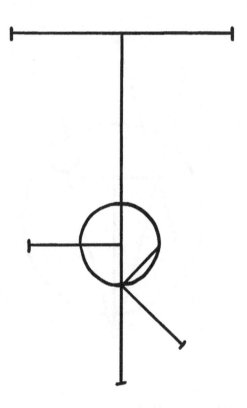

TAROT READINGS AID

This sigil can be used as a preparatory step prior to a Tarot reading or on general as a means of improvement. It helps by clearing the mind and providing the proper mental environment for clear and accurate readings.

Mantra: FORTENT GAI

Miscellaneous Sigils

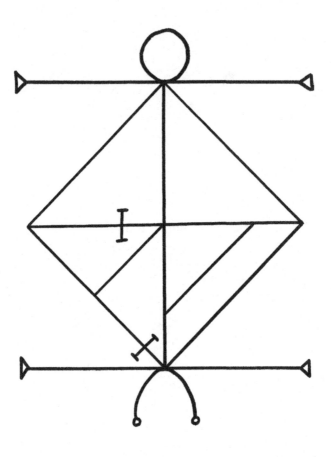

FOR POSITIVITY

Use this sigil when a positive mindset is needed. It can be adapted to any occasion and magickal work.

Mantra: SVERN BYOPT GHUJIC

Notes:

FOR NEGATIVITY

Use this sigil when a negative mindset is needed. It is very helpful for when one needs to avoid certain situations or choices that seem pleasing but are certain to have negative outcomes.

Mantra: SVUNGER THO JABYC

83

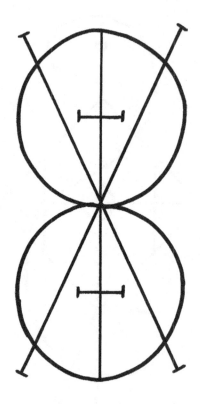

TO FAVOUR PROBABILITIES

Use this sigil for when better chances are needed. Use it to manipulate probabilities and the outcome of certaini actions and choices.

Mantra: GERVUD TIB PALFOS

Notes:

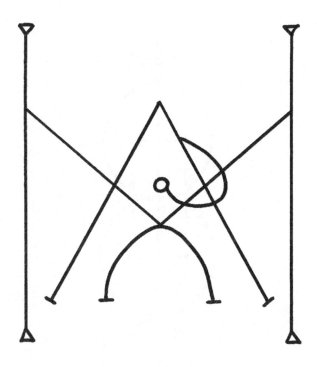

TO ENHANCE THE CURRENT STATE OF LUCK

This sigil can be used to amplify the feeling and overall luck in its current state. Make the lucky luckier and the un-lucky unluckier.

Mantra: HAR MUNTYC LEK

Notes:

85

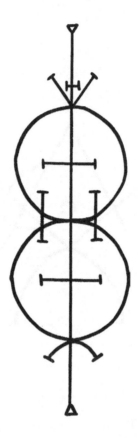

TO RECOGNISE PROBABILITIES

This sigil provides a clear and focuses state of mind that makes it easier to spot great chances or foresee the probably outcomes of certain acts, choices, events and situations.

Mantra: PHERLING BOSTA

Notes:

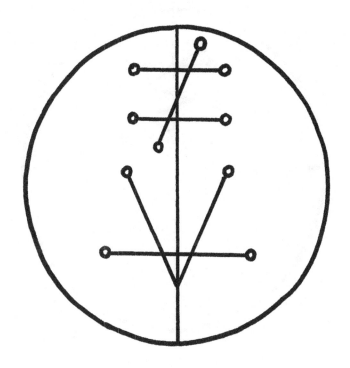

GENERAL HEALING AID

Use this sigil to get better chances of a proper and faster healing process. It works by making the brain focusing more in the procedures and the production of substances needed for physical healing.

Mantra: GALINHED

Notes:

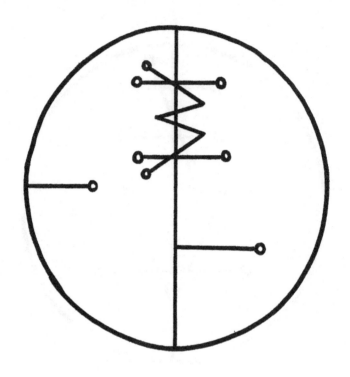

MENTAL HEALING

This sigil can be used when one needs to heal their mind. This can be an obsession, stress caused from over-thinking, mental trauma caused by a traumatic experience and more.

Mantra: LENHIGTAM

Notes:

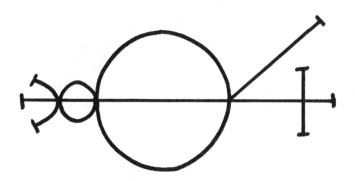

TO PROMOTE INSPIRATION

Use this sigil when feeling stuck and in need of new ideas. This can be called the "muse" sigil as it works by arousing the parts of brain that are responsible for creativity, imagination and processing.

Mantra: MONIS PARTE

Notes:

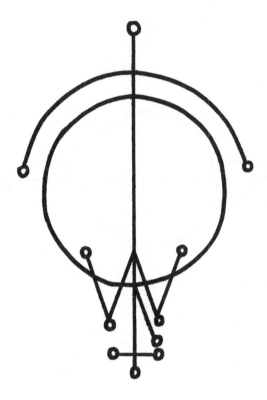

TO PROMOTE CREATIVITY

Use this sigil when a creative boost is needed. It works by sparking up the brain centers that are responsible for creative thoughts and productivity.

Mantra: MARCIT EVOY

Notes:

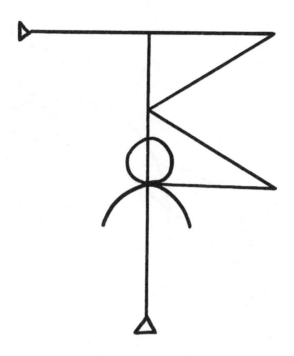

TO PROMOTE ELOQUENCE

This sigil can be used when an advanced verbal ability is needed, such as in court cases, public debates or general persuasion.

It works by triggering the part of the brain that is responsible for verbal communication.

Mantra: LENTO BUQ

Notes:

91

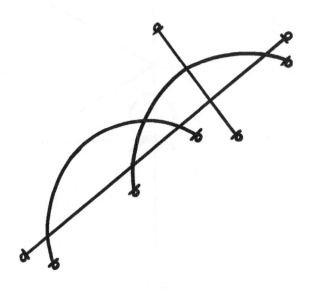

TO PROMOTE DETERMINATION

Use this sigil when feeling indecisive towards taking action or feeling a general lack of determination in certain tasks.

Mantra: BER MINDT

Notes:

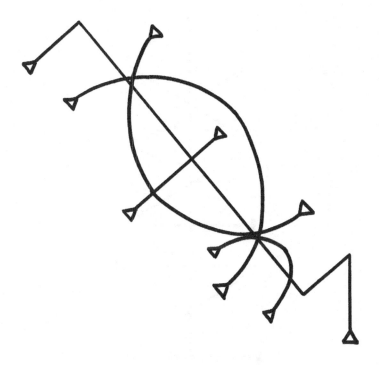

TO PROMOTE CALMNESS

When agitated or restless, one can use this sigil as an aid in order to find calmness. It is a great addition to physical and mental techniques such as yoga and general meditation.

This sigil can also be used frequently as a means to promote calmness in general in one's life.

Mantra: CELMBA

Notes:

93

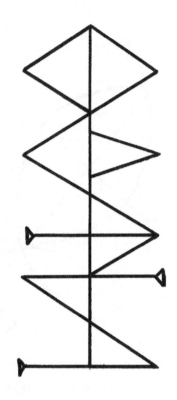

TO PROMOTE CONFIDENCE

This sigil can help one achieve a desirable state of confidence by promoting the existing levels of confidence no matter how small they are.

It is best to be used frequently.

Mantra: CEBD FONTI

Notes:

FOR FRIENDSHIP

This sigil can be used in all matters that deal with friendship. From reconciliation and finding friends to cutting ties and magickal workings that involve friendship.

Mantra: PARSH FEIND

Notes:

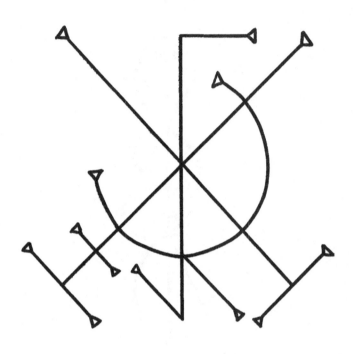

FOR THE TRUTH

This is a sigil that can be used in many cases. Its main function is to aid spells and rituals that are made to reveal the truth, but it can also be used as a mental push to help someone find the way and admit the truth to another person.

Mantra: DRENT SULHAF

Notes:

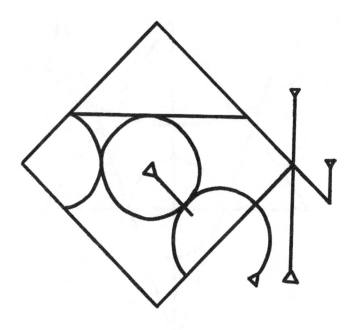

FOR STIMULATION

This sigil can be used to create and and promote any kind of stimulation, physical, mental, emotional, spiritual, magickal etc.

Mantra: NARET GIMOLULS

Notes:

FOR COMFORT

Use this sigil when the feeling of comfort is needed. this can be either physical comfort or mental.

Mantra: GNARLOC FIEMT

Notes:

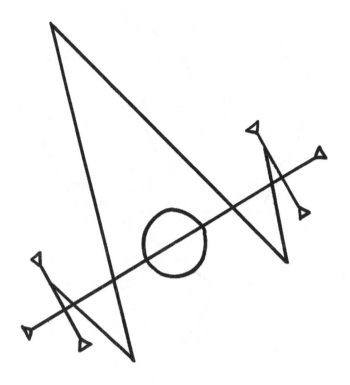

TO BANISH NEGATIVITY

This sigil can be used in order to banish all negative thoughts and feelings from one's mind. It also helps alleviate the mental pain caused by emotional strain.

Mantra: VESHTA

Notes:

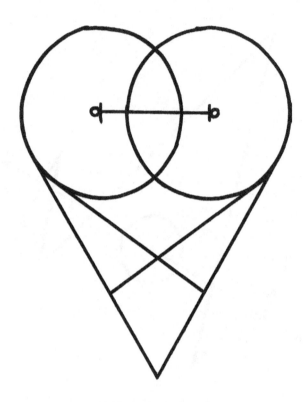

TO INSTILL THE LOVE OF LEARNING

Use this sigil when an extra motivation for learning is needed. Some times we need an extra push and motivation in order to make the decision and start learning new things such as general knowledge and new skills.

Mantra: NARGOL VEI

Notes:

NOTES:

PHYSICAL SIGILS

The Physical Sigils or "Seals of Power" have to carved, drawn, places or by any other means used on physical objects.

On each page, you will find a sigil in its visual form and its denomination.

Sigils for Protection

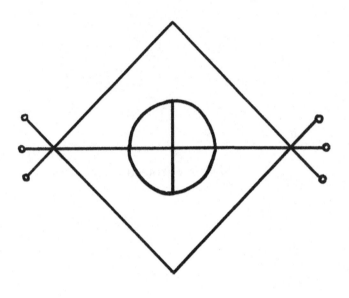

PROTECTION (in general)

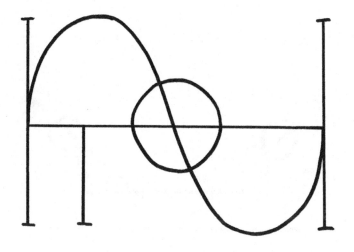

PROTECTION FROM JINXES

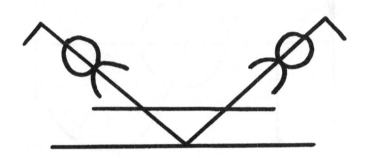

PROTECTION FROM OFFENSIVE MAGICK

Note: It will also block the offensive magick of the user.

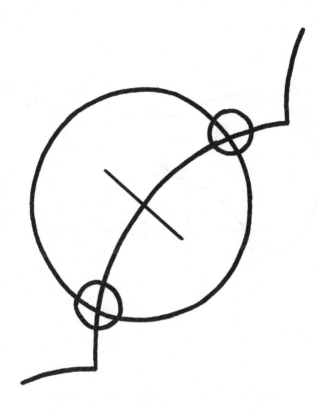

PROTECTION FROM MALEVOLENT SPIRITS

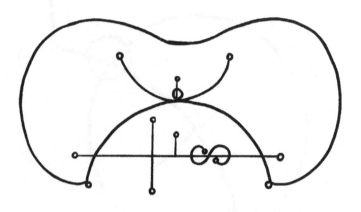

PROTECTION FROM BAD DREAMS

TO PROTECT A HOME

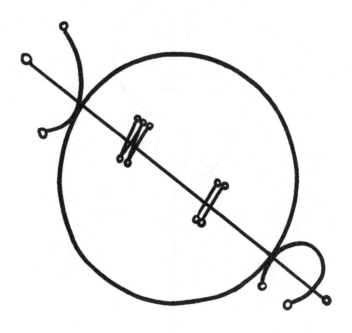

TO PROTECT A PERSON

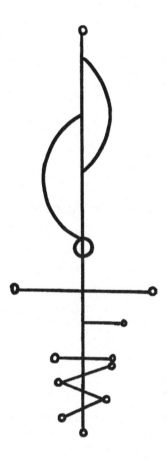

TO PROTECT A SPACE, AREA, ROOM etc.

Sigils for Divination

They can be used on mats, cards, talismans etc.

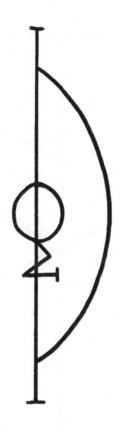

GENERAL DIVINATION AID

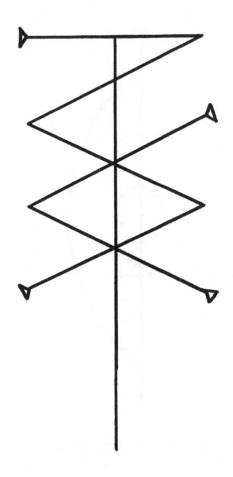

DIVINATION: TAROT

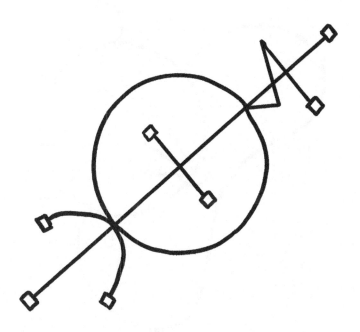

DIVINATION: RUNES

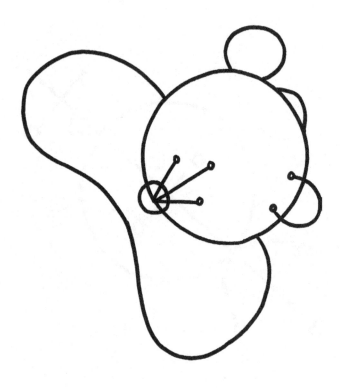

DIVINATION: PROPHETIC DREAMS

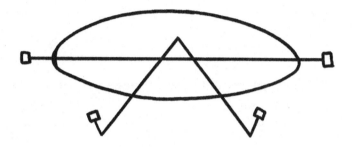

DIVINATION: GEOMANCY

Sigils to be used during:

Spells, rituals and other magickal workings.

CANDLE MAGICK

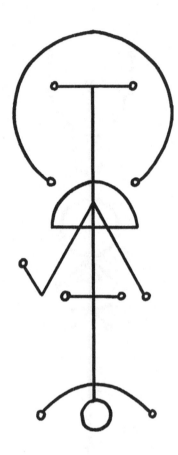

CANDLE CHARGING

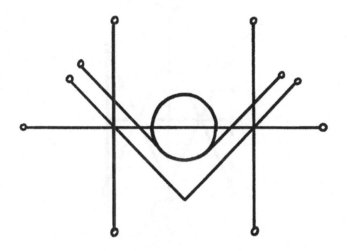

HERBAL CHARGING

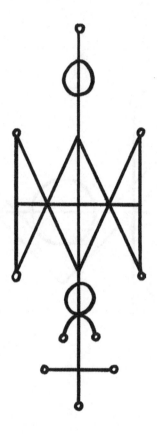

MANIFESTATION

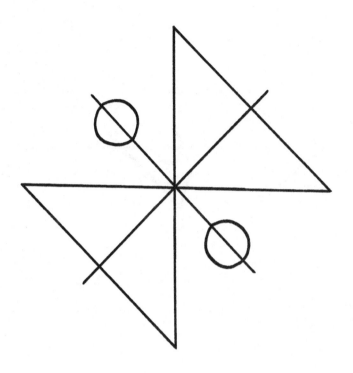

PROTECTION

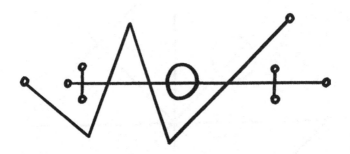

HEALING

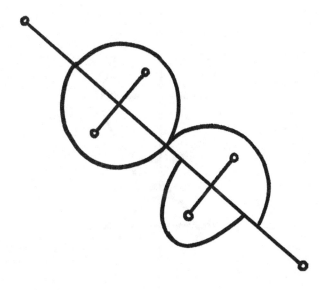

LUST

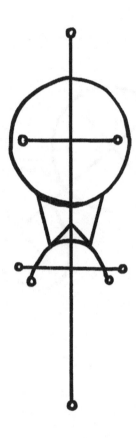

CHARMWORK

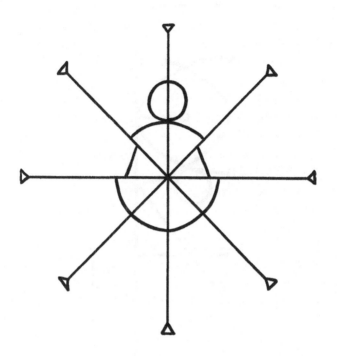

JINXES

GLAMOUR

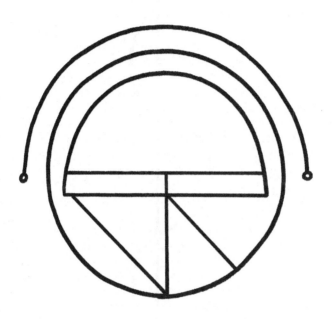

CONCEALING

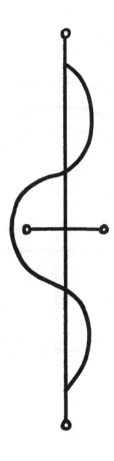

BINDING

PROSPERITY

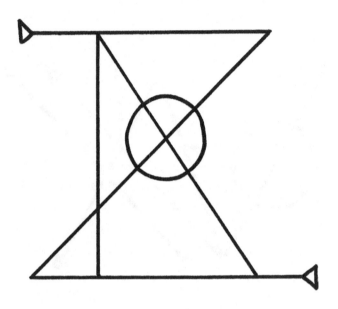

STRENGTH

EMPOWERMENT

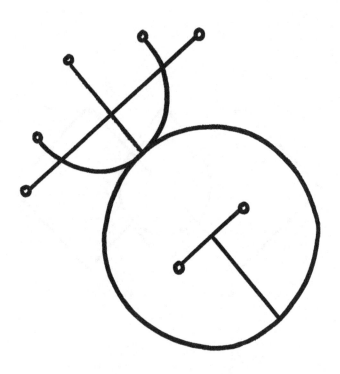

CLEANSING

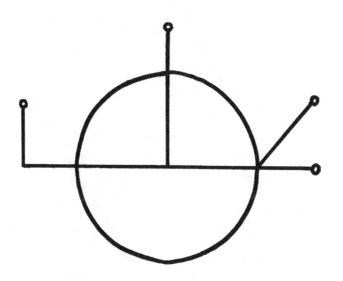

OFFERING

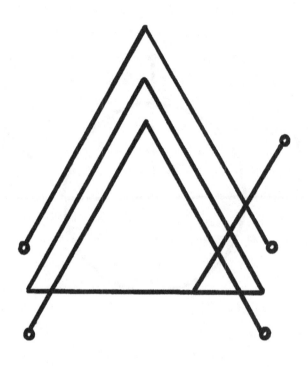

ELEMENTAL MAGICK: AIR

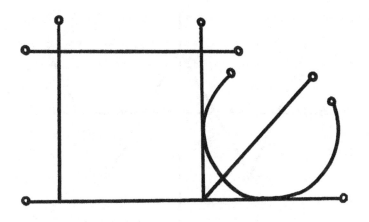

ELEMENTAL MAGICK: FIRE

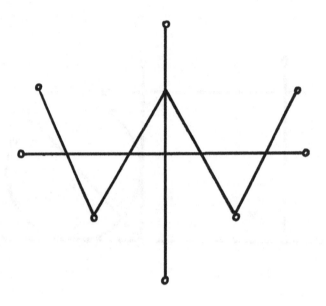

ELEMENTAL MAGICK: WATER

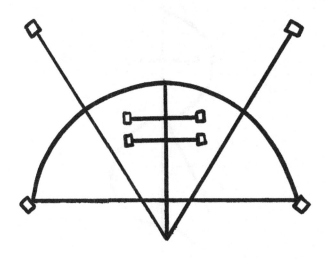

ELEMENTAL MAGICK: EARTH

ELEMENTAL MAGICK: SPIRIT

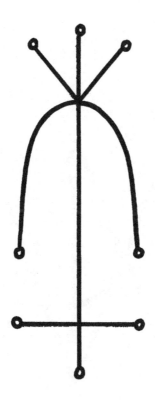

LUCK

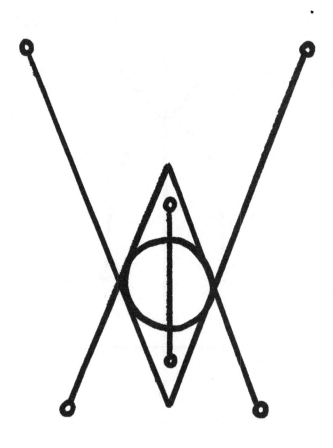

INVOCATION

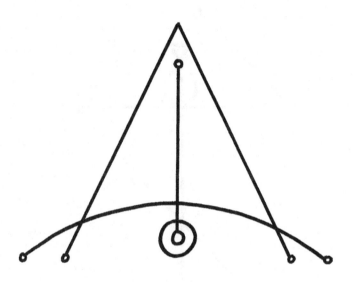

EVOCATION

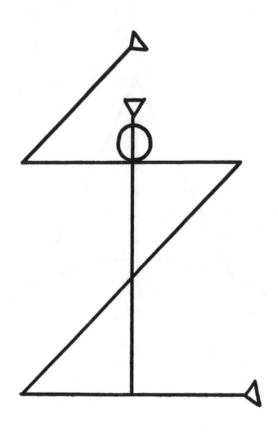

SUMMONING

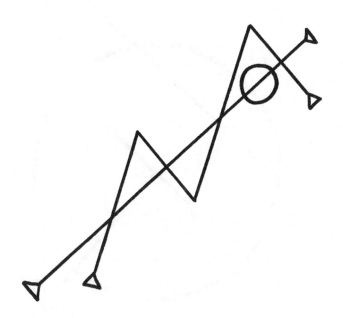

BANISHING

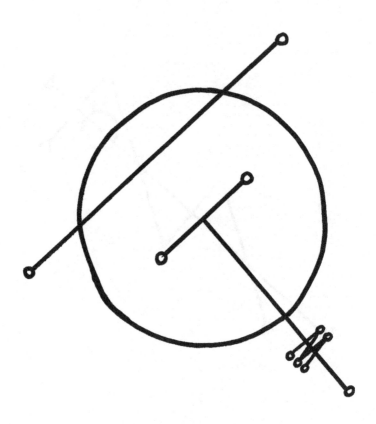

EMOTIONS

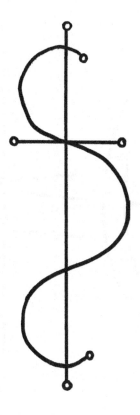

SPIRITUALITY

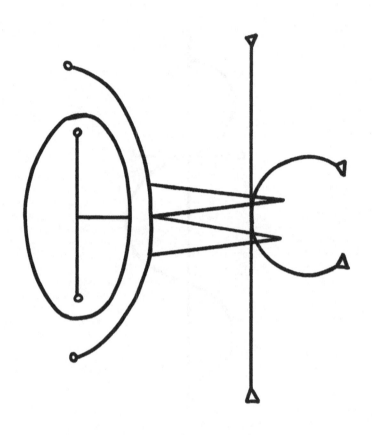

COUNTER MAGICK

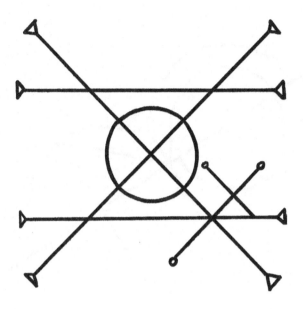

HEX BREAKING

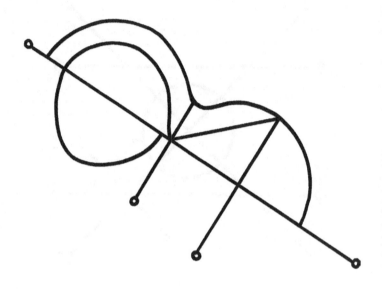

BIRTH RITUALS

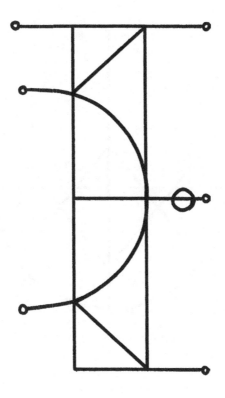

MARRIAGE RITUALS

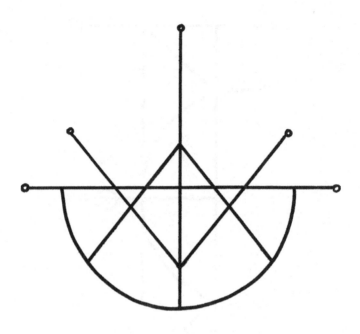

DEATH RITUALS

POTENCY

NOTES:

NOTES:

Made in the USA
Las Vegas, NV
30 January 2024